Edmund J. (Edmund Janes) James, Bundesverfassung
Switzerland.

Federal Constitution of Switzerland

Edmund J. (Edmund Janes) James, Bundesverfassung Switzerland.

Federal Constitution of Switzerland

ISBN/EAN: 9783337151447

Printed in Europe, USA, Canada, Australia, Japan

Cover: Foto ©Suzi / pixelio.de

More available books at **www.hansebooks.com**

PUBLICATIONS

OF THE

UNIVERSITY OF PENNSYLVANIA.

POLITICAL ECONOMY AND PUBLIC LAW SERIES.

EDMUND J. JAMES, Ph.D., Editor.

NO. 8.

THE FEDERAL CONSTITUTION

OF

SWITZERLAND.

TRANSLATED

BY

EDMUND J. JAMES, Ph.D.,

Professor in the University of Pennsylvania.

PHILADELPHIA.

1890.

For Sale by Porter and Coates, Philadelphia.

PRICE FIFTY CENTS.

INDEX TO CONSTITUTION.

(3)

THE FEDERAL CONSTITUTION

OF

SWITZERLAND.

PREAMBLE.

In the Name of Almighty God!

The Swiss Confederation,

For the purpose of strengthening the Union of the Allies and of preserving and promoting the unity, power and honor of the Swiss Nation, has adopted the following Federal Constitution:

THE FEDERAL CONSTITUTION

OF THE

SWISS ~~CON~~FEDERATION.

FIRST DIVISION.

GENERAL PROVISIONS.

ARTICLE 1.

The peoples of the twenty-two sovereign Cantons associated in the present Union, viz: Zurich, Bern, Luzern, Uri, Schwyz, Unterwalden (Upper and Lower), Glarus, Zug, Freiburg, Solothurn, Basel (City and Country), Schaffhausen, Appenzell (the two Rhodes), St.-Gallen, Grisons, Aargau, Thurgau, Ticino, Vaud, Valais, Neuchâtel, and Geneva, taken together, form the SWISS CONFEDERATION.

ARTICLE 2.

The purpose of the Union is: the maintenance of national independence, establishment of tranquillity and order within the country, protection of freedom, and of the rights of the Allies, and the promotion of their common welfare.

ARTICLE 3.

The Cantons are sovereign, so far as their sovereignty is not restricted by the Federal Constitution, and as such they

(11)

may exercise all rights which are not delegated to the Federal Power.

ARTICLE 4.

All Swiss shall be equal before the law. In Switzerland there shall be no subjects, nor any privileges of place, birth, family or person.

ARTICLE 5.

The Union guarantees to the Cantons their territory, their sovereignty within the limits set by Article 3, their constitutions, liberty, the rights of the people, the constitutional rights of the citizens, and the rights and privileges which the people may have conferred upon their public authorities.

ARTICLE 6.

The Cantons are required to demand of the Union its guaranty for their constitutions.

The Union shall accord this guaranty, provided :

a. That they contain nothing contrary to the provisions of the Federal Constitution.

b. That they provide for the exercise of political rights according to Republican (either representative or democratic) forms.

c. That they have been accepted by the people and can be revised whenever an absolute majority of the citizens demand it.

ARTICLE 7.

All special alliances or treaties of a political character between the various Cantons are forbidden.

The Cantons, however, shall have the right to make agreements with one another on subjects pertaining to legislation, justice and administration : such agreements, however, shall be submitted to the Federal authority, which may forbid their execution, if they contain anything contrary to the Union or to the rights of other Cantons. If such agreements are not open to these objections, the respective Cantons may demand the coöperation of the Federal authorities in their execution.

ARTICLE 8.

The Union shall have the sole power to declare war, conclude peace, and enter into alliances or treaties, especially customs and commercial treaties with foreign countries.

ARTICLE 9.

In exceptional cases the Cantons may enter into treaties with foreign countries concerning matters of the public economy, of vicinage, and of police : but such treaties shall not contain anything contrary to the Union or the rights of other Cantons.

ARTICLE 10.

Official intercourse between the Cantons and foreign governments or their representatives shall take place through the Federal Council. But the Cantons may deal directly with the subordinate authorities and officers of a foreign state in regard to matters mentioned in Article 9.

ARTICLE 11.

Military capitulations are absolutely prohibited.*

ARTICLE 12.

Members of the Federal Government, civil and military officials of the Union, and Federal representatives or commissioners, shall not accept from foreign governments any pension, salary, title, present or decoration.

If they are already in possession of pensions, titles or decorations, they shall be required to refuse the pension and refrain from bearing either title or decoration during their term of office.

The Federal Council may, however, permit subordinate officers and appointees to continue to draw their pensions.

* i. e. Agreements to furnish soldiers to foreign countries.

Decorations shall not be worn in the Swiss Army, nor shall titles conferred by foreign governments be borne.

Every officer, under-officer and soldier shall be forbidden to accept any such distinction.

ARTICLE 13.

The Union shall not be allowed to maintain a standing army.

Without permission of the Federal Government no Canton, or in the case of Divided Cantons, no Half-Canton, shall be permitted to keep more than 300 permanent troops, exclusive of the gendarmes.

ARTICLE 14.

The Cantons are prohibited, in case of disputes arising between them, from arming and from all attempts to enforce their own rights, but such dispute shall be submitted to Federal decision.

ARTICLE 15.

If sudden danger threaten any Canton from foreign countries, the government of the endangered Canton shall call upon the other Cantons for help, and notify the Federal Government, at the same time, without prejudice however to the later measures of the same. The Cantons so summoned are bound to come to its aid. The costs shall be borne by the Union.

ARTICLE 16.

When internal order is disturbed or when danger threatens from another Canton, the government of the endangered Canton shall immediately notify the Federal Council, in order that it may take the necessary measures within the limits of its competence (Article 102, Nos. 3, 10 and 11), or may summon the Federal Assembly. In urgent cases the Cantonal government concerned, notifying the Federal Government of its action, may summon other Cantons to its aid, to which the latter are bound to respond.

If the Cantonal Government is unable to call for aid, the competent Federal authority may interfere on its own initiative, and if the safety of Switzerland be endangered, it shall be its duty to do so.

In cases of Federal intervention the Federal authorities shall secure the observance of the provisions of Article 5.

The costs shall be borne by the Canton calling for or compelling intervention, unless the Federal Assembly, on account of peculiar circumstances, shall decide otherwise.

ARTICLE 17.

In the cases mentioned in Articles 15 and 16, every Canton shall permit free passage to the troops through its territory. The troops shall be immediately placed under Federal control.

ARTICLE 18.

Every Swiss is subject to military service. Soldiers who lose their lives or suffer permanent injury to their health in the Federal military service shall be entitled in case of need to Federal support for themselves or families.

Soldiers shall in the first instance be equipped, clothed and armed at public expense. The arms shall remain in possession of the soldier under such conditions as Federal law shall provide.

The Union shall make uniform laws on the subject of fees for exemption from military service.

ARTICLE 19.

The Federal Army shall consist (a) of the standing contingents of the Cantons; (b), of all Swiss who though not belonging to the standing troops are yet subject to military service.

The control of the Federal Army, together with all the materials for or belonging thereto, shall be an affair of the Union.

In times of danger the Union shall have the exclusive.

and immediate control over all troops, whether incorporated in the Federal Army or not, and over all other military resources of the Cantons.

The Cantons may exercise control over the military resources of their territory so far as they are not limited by the constitutional or legal regulations of the Union.

ARTICLE 20.

Military legislation is an affair of the Union. The execution of the military laws within the Cantons shall take place by the Cantonal authorities under the supervision of the Union, and according to regulations made by Federal law.

The entire military instruction and the arming of the troops shall be under the control of the Union.

The clothing and equipments and the subsistence of the troops shall be provided by the Cantons; but the costs thereof shall be returned to the Cantons by the Union in a manner to be determined by Federal law.

ARTICLE 21.

So far as military considerations shall not forbid, the various corps shall consist of men from the same Canton.

The composition of such corps, the duty of preserving their efficiency, and the appointment and promotion of the officers, shall be reserved to the Cantons, subject to general rules to be established by the Union.

ARTICLE 22.

Upon giving fair compensation, the Union shall have the right to take either for use or as property the parade grounds and buildings used for military purposes, together with all their belongings, in the various Cantons.

The system of fixing the compensation shall be determined by Federal law.

ARTICLE 23.

The Union may, in the interest of the Confederation, or of a large part of the same, undertake public works at the expense of the Confederation, or may assist in their construction.

For this purpose it may exercise the right of expropriation upon making full compensation. The special provisions on this subject shall be left to Federal legislation.

The Federal Assembly may forbid the construction of public works whenever they would endanger the military interest of the Confederation.

ARTICLE 24.

To the Union shall belong the general supervision of the water and forest police measures in the mountains.

It shall assist in the correction and control of the mountain streams and in the afforesting of their sources, and shall prescribe the necessary protective regulations for the preservation of such works and of the forests now existing.

ARTICLE 25.

The Union is authorized to adopt regulations as to the exercise of the right of hunting and fishing, especially for the preservation of the nobler sorts of game, and for the protection of birds which are useful to agriculture or forestry.

ARTICLE 26.

Legislation pertaining to the construction and management of railways is an affair of the Union.

ARTICLE 27.

The Union may establish, in addition to the existing Polytechnic School, a University and other higher institutions of learning, or may assist in the support of such institutions.

The Cantons shall provide for satisfactory primary instruction. which shall be solely under public supervision. Such instruction shall be obligatory, and in the public schools free of charge.

The public schools shall be open to the adherents of all faiths, without prejudice to their freedom of belief or of conscience.

The Union shall take such measures as may seem necessary against Cantons which do not conform to these provisions.

ARTICLE 28.

The system of customs duties is a Federal affair. The Union may collect import and export duties.

ARTICLE 29.

In the collection of customs duties the following provisions shall be observed:

1. Import duties.

a. The raw material necessary for domestic industry or agriculture shall be taxed at as low a rate as possible.

b. Likewise all articles which may be classed as necessaries of life.

c. Articles of luxury shall pay the highest rates.

The foregoing principles are to be observed in the conclusion of commercial treaties with foreign countries so far as possible.

2. Export duties are to be fixed at as low a rate as possible.

3. The necessary regulations as to intercourse along the frontier and at the markets shall be incorporated in the customs tariff legislation. The Union may at any time under extraordinary circumstances adopt temporary measures in conflict with the foregoing principles.

ARTICLE 30.

The income from customs shall flow into the Federal Treasury.

The compensations which have hitherto been paid to the Cantons in lieu of the customs, road and bridge tolls, market fees, and similar items, are hereby abolished.

As an exceptional indemnity the Cantons Uri, Grisons, Ticino and Valais, in consideration of their international Alpine highways, shall receive a yearly compensation which in view of all circumstances is fixed as follows:

For Uri . . . . Francs. 80,000.
" Grisons . . . . " . 200,000.
" Ticino . . . . " 200,000.
" Valais . . . . " 50,000.

For breaking roads through the snow on the St. Gothard, the Cantons Uri and Ticino shall receive a yearly compensation of 40,000 francs, all told, until the road over the pass is replaced by a railway.

ARTICLE 31.

The freedom of trade and of industry throughout the whole extent of the Confederation is hereby guaranteed. Excepted from this rule are:

a. The salt and tobacco monopoly, the Federal customs, the import duties on wine and spirituous liquors, as well as the other taxes on consumable commodities expressly recognized by the Union according to the provisions of Article 32.

b. Sanitary police regulations against epidemics and veterinary diseases.

c. Regulations as to exercise of trade and industry, as to taxation of business and the use of streets.

But such regulations must not interfere with the principle of freedom of trade and commerce.

ARTICLE 32.

The cantons may collect import duties on wine and other spirituous liquors mentioned in Article 31, *a, b* and *c,* under the following conditions:

a. In the collection of such duties, free transit of goods shall be interfered with in no way; and, in general, trade shall be hindered as little as possible, and burdened with no other duties.

b. If the articles imported for use are again exported, the duties so paid shall be refunded without further charges.

c. The products of Swiss industry shall be taxed at a lower rate than those of foreign origin.

d. Import duties on wine and other spiritious liquors of Swiss origin shall not be increased where they now exist, nor be introduced into Cantons which do not levy such dues.*

e. The laws and ordinances of the Cantons in reference to such import duties shall be submitted for approval to the Federal authorities before going into effect, so that neglect of the foregoing provisions may be prevented.

With the close of the year 1890 all import duties which may be levied at that time by the Cantons, as well as all similar duties raised by individual communities, shall be abolished without compensation.

ARTICLE 33.

The Cantons may make the practice of the liberal professions dependent upon giving evidence of fitness.

Federal legislation shall provide a means of obtaining certificates of such fitness, which shall be valid throughout the whole Confederation.

ARTICLE 34.

The Union may pass uniform laws as to the employment of children in factories and the length of the working day for adults in the same. It is also authorized to issue regulations for the protection of laborers in dangerous or unhealthful employments.

---

* The manufacture and sale of spirituous liquors was made a federal monopoly October 25, 1885.

The business of emigration agents and of private insurance companies shall be subject to the supervision and legislation of the Union.

ARTICLE 35.

The establishment of gambling houses is prohibited. Those now in existence shall be closed by the 31st December, 1877.

All concessions granted or renewed since the beginning of the year 1871 are hereby declared null and void.

The Union may also take proper measures in regard to lotteries.

ARTICLE 36.

The post and telegraph throughout the whole extent of the Confederation belong to the Union.

The income from the administration of post and telegraph shall belong to the Federal Treasury.

The tariff of charges shall be regulated throughout the territory of the Confederation according to uniform principles in as equitable a manner as possible.

The inviolability of postal and telegraph secrecy is guaranteed.

ARTICLE 37.

The Union shall exercise general supervision over the roads and bridges in whose maintenance the Union may have an interest.

The moneys which according to Article 30 belong to certain Cantons in view of their international Alpine highways shall be retained by the Federal authorities in case these roads are not kept in good condition by the respective Cantons.

ARTICLE 38.

To the Union shall belong the exercise of all rights included in the coinage monopoly.

The Union alone shall coin money.

It shall determine the monetary system and prescribe regulations for the valuation of foreign coin.

ARTICLE 39.

The Union is authorized to make general regulations by federal law as to the issue and redemption of bank notes.

It shall not, however, establish any monopoly for the issue of bank notes, nor make them a legal tender. .

ARTICLE 40.

The establishment of weights and measures is an affair of the Union. ·

The execution of laws relating to this subject shall be undertaken by the Cantons under the supervision of the Union.

ARTICLE 41.

The manufacture and sale of gunpowder throughout the whole territory of the Confederation belongs solely to the Union.

Blasting materials not usable as gunpowder are not included in this monopoly.

ARTICLE 42.

The expenditures of the Union shall be defrayed :

a. From the proceeds of Federal property.

b. From the proceeds of Federal frontier duties.

c. From the proceeds of the post and telegraph.

d. From the proceeds of the powder monopoly.

e. From the proceeds of half the gross income from the fees for exemption from military service received by the Cantons.

f. From the contributions of the Cantons, to be determined by federal legislation according to the taxable resources of the Cantons, upon as equitable a basis as possible.

ARTICLE 43.

Every citizen of a Canton is also a Swiss citizen.

As such (after furnishing evidence of his right to vote) he can take part at his place of residence in all Federal elections and votes.

No one shall exercise political rights in more than one Canton.

Every Swiss citizen shall enjoy at his place of residence all rights of the citizens of the Canton, as also all rights of the citizens of the commune.

He shall, however, have no share in the common property of citizens or of the corporation, nor shall he exercise the right to vote in matters pertaining purely to such affairs, unless the Cantonal laws determine otherwise.

In Cantonal and commercial matters he shall acquire the right to vote by a residence of three months.

The Cantonal laws in relation to settlement and the right to vote of those who settle in the communes are subject to the approval of the Federal Council.

ARTICLE 44.

No Canton shall expel a Cantonal citizen from its territory or deprive him of the right of citizenship.

The conditions on which foreigners may be admitted to Swiss citizenship, as well as those under which a Swiss may renounce his citizenship for the sake of acquiring a foreign citizenship, shall be determined by Federal legislation.

ARTICLE 45.

Every Swiss shall have the right to settle at any place within Swiss territory if he possesses a certificate of origin or some similar paper.

In exceptional cases, the right of settlement may be refused to those who in consequence of criminal sentence are not in possession of the rights and dignity of citizenship, or it may be withdrawn from such.

The right of settlement may, moreover, be withdrawn from those who in consequence of serious misdemeanors have been repeatedly punished, as also from those who become a permanent burden upon public charity, and whose native commune or Canton refuses to give adequate assistance, in spite of official notification to do so.

In Cantons where the system of local relief obtains, the permission of settlement for natives of the Canton may be made dependent on the condition that the parties are able to work and have not hitherto been a permanent burden upon public charity in their previous place of residence.

Every expulsion on account of poverty must be approved by the Cantonal government, and notice must first be sent to the government of the Canton of which the person expelled is a native.

No Swiss citizen may be burdened by the Canton which may permit him to settle within its bounds by the requirement of security or any other special burdens connected with settlement. Nor shall the commune in which he settles tax him in any different way from its own native citizens.

A Federal law shall fix the maximum sum which may be taken as registration fee for the privilege of settling.

ARTICLE 46.

With regard to the civil relations, those who have settled in a place shall be subject as a rule to the rights and legislation of the place of residence.

Federal law shall determine the application of this principle, and shall also make the necessary regulations to prevent double taxation.

ARTICLE 47.

A Federal law shall define the difference between settlement and sojourn, and also prescribe the regulations as to the political and civil rights of sojourners.

ARTICLE 48.

A Federal law shall make provision as to the cost of the

care and burial of poor citizens of one Canton who may become sick or die in another Canton.

ARTICLE 49.

The freedom of faith and conscience shall be inviolable.

No one shall be compelled to take part in any religious society or in any religious instruction, or to undertake any religious act, nor shall he be punished in any way whatever for his religious views.

The religious education of children to the close of their 16th year shall be under the control of father or guardian, subject to the principles enumerated above.

The exercise of civil or political rights shall not be abridged by any conditions or provisions of a confessional or religious nature.

Religious views shall not absolve from the performance of civil duties.

No one shall be required to pay taxes which are levied specially for the purely religious purposes of any religious society to which he does not belong. The exact application of this principle shall be determined by Federal legislation.

ARTICLE 50.

The free exercise of religion is guaranteed, within the limits of morality and public order.

The Cantons and the Union shall have the right to take necessary measures for the establishment of order and public peace among the adherents of the various religious societies, as well as against any interference in the rights of citizens or of the State by church authorities.

Disputes within either the field of public or private law arising from the formation or division of religious societies may be brought before the proper Federal authorities for decision by means of formal complaint.

The establishment of bishoprics on Swiss soil is subject to Federal approval.

ARTICLE 51.

Neither the Society of Jesus nor any allied Society shall be suffered in any part of Switzerland, and all participation of their members either in church or school is prohibited. This prohibition may also be extended by Federal law to other religious orders whose action is dangerous to the state or tends to destroy the peace between the various confessions.

ARTICLE 52.

The establishment of new, or the restoration of disestablished, monasteries or orders is forbidden.

ARTICLE 53.

The determination and certification of facts of the civil state belongs to the civil authorities. More exact regulations shall be made by Federal law.

The disposition of burial places shall belong to the civil authorities. It is their duty to see that every one can be decently buried.

ARTICLE 54.

The right of marriage shall be under the protection of the Union.

This right shall not be limited for confessional or economic considerations, nor on account of previous conduct or other police reasons.

All marriages contracted in a Canton or in a foreign country according to the laws there prevailing shall be recognized as marriage within the territory of the Confederation.

By marriage the wife acquires the right of domicile and settlement belonging to the man.

By subsequent marriage of the parents, children are rendered legitimate who were born before marriage.

All collection of bridal settlement fees and similar taxes is prohibited.

ARTICLE 55.

Freedom of the press is guaranteed.

Cantonal legislation shall provide for all abuse of the same, but such legislation shall be subject to the approval of the Federal Council.

The Union may issue regulations against the abuse of the freedom of the press when it is directed against the Union or its officers.

ARTICLE 56.

The citizens shall have the right to form associations, so far as they are not either in their purpose or methods illegal or dangerous to the State. The abuse of this right may be prevented by Cantonal legislation.

ARTICLE 57.

The right of petition is guaranteed.

ARTICLE 58.

No one shall be deprived of his constitutional judge, and there shall consequently be no exceptional courts.

Ecclesiastical jurisdiction is hereby abolished.

ARTICLE 59.

A solvent debtor with a permanent residence in Switzerland must be summoned in personal suits before a judge of his own place of residence, and the property of such a person (outside of the Canton in which he lives) can not be seized or sequestered for claims against him.

Provided that with reference to foreigners the provisions of the respective international treaties shall apply.

Imprisonment for debt is hereby abolished.

ARTICLE 60.

All Cantons are required to treat all Swiss citizens like their own citizens, both in their legislation and in judicial procedure.

ARTICLE 61.

Valid judgments in civil cases which have been given in one Canton may be enforced anywhere in Switzerland.

ARTICLE 62.

All internal taxes on property leaving one Canton for another (abzugsrechte, la traite foraine) are hereby abolished as likewise all rights of first purchase (zugrechte, droit de retrait), of citizens of one Canton against those of another Canton.*

ARTICLE 63.

The right of free emigration to foreign states shall be recognized so far as this is reciprocal.

ARTICLE 64.

The Union shall have power to legislate :

1. Upon civil capacity.

2. Upon all legal relations referring to trade and mobiliary transactions, (law of obligations, including commercial law and law of promissory notes).

3. Upon authors' property in works of literature and art, upon executionary procedure for debts, and upon the law of bankruptcy.†

The administration of the laws shall belong to the Cantons, except so much as may be assigned to the Federal Tribunal.

ARTICLE 65.

No sentence of death shall be pronounced for political offenses.

Corporal punishments are hereby forbidden.

---

* It was customary formerly to deduct from 5 to 10% from all property going out of the Canton by inheritance or marriage (abzugsrecht) It was also usual when a person wished to sell land, to recognize a right in his relatives or even neighbors or fellow citizens of the Canton to take the property at an arbitrated value (zugrecht).

† July 10, 1887, this clause was practically amended by the acceptance of a patent law.

ARTICLE 66.

Federal law shall determine the conditions in which a Swiss citizen may be declared to have forfeited his political rights.

ARTICLE 67.

Federal law shall prescribe the necessary regulations as to the extradition by one Canton to another of accused persons, but such extradition shall not be made compulsory for political offenses or offenses against the press laws.

ARTICLE 68.

Federal legislation shall determine the civil rights of people without a domicile, and shall take measures to prevent the rise of such classes.

ARTICLE 69.

The Union shall have power to legislate upon the sanitary regulations to be adopted against dangerous epidemics and veterinary diseases.

ARTICLE 70.

The Union may expel from Swiss territory all foreigners who endanger the internal or external safety of the Confederation.

SECOND DIVISION.

FEDERAL AUTHORITIES.

I. FEDERAL ASSEMBLY.

ARTICLE 71.

Excepting the rights of the people and the Cantons (Articles 89 and 121), the supreme authority of the Union shall be exercised by the Federal Assembly, which shall consist of two divisions:

A. The National Council.

B. The Council of States.

A. *The National Council.*

ARTICLE 72.

The National Council shall consist of representatives of the Swiss People. One member shall be chosen for every 20,000 of the whole population. *2 2, ↽-◡-◡*

A fraction of more than 10,000 souls shall be counted as 20,000.

Every Canton, and in the Divided Cantons each division thereof, shall choose at least one member.

ARTICLE 73.

The elections for the National Council shall be direct. They shall take place within Federal districts, but no district shall include portions of two different Cantons.

ARTICLE 74.

Every male Swiss who has completed his 20th year, and who is not excluded from the active right of citizenship according to the laws of the Canton where he resides, shall be entitled to take part in elections and votes.

The Union may, however, pass uniform laws as to the right to vote.

ARTICLE 75.

Every male Swiss citizen being a layman and a voter is eligible as member of the National Council.

ARTICLE 76.

The National Council shall be elected for three years, the term of all members expiring at the same time.

ARTICLE 77.

Members of the Council of States or of the Federal Council, or officers appointed by the latter, shall not be at the same time members of the National Council.

ARTICLE 78.

The National Council shall choose from among its members a President and a Vice President for each ordinary and extraordinary session.

The member who has filled the office of President for one ordinary session is not eligible either for President or Vice President of the ordinary session immediately following. Nor can the same person be Vice President for two consecutive ordinary sessions.

The President shall have the casting vote in case of a tie: in elections he votes as any other member.

ARTICLE 79.

The members of the National Council shall receive a compensation from the Federal Treasury.

B. The Council of States.

ARTICLE 80.

The Council of States shall consist of forty-four representatives of the Cantons. Each Canton shall elect two representatives, and in the divided Cantons each division shall elect one.

ARTICLE 81.

No member of the National Council or of the Federal Council shall be at the same time a member of the Council of States.

ARTICLE 82.

The Council of States shall elect from among its members a President and a Vice President for each ordinary and extraordinary session.

From among the representatives of that Canton from which a president has been chosen for an ordinary session, neither the President or Vice President can be taken for the next following ordinary session.

Representatives of the same Canton shall not fill the office of Vice President during two consecutive ordinary sessions.

The President may give the casting vote in case of a tie: in elections he votes as any other member.

ARTICLE 83.

Members of the Council of States shall be compensated by their respective Cantons.

C. Powers of the Federal Assembly.

ARTICLE 84.

The National Council and the Council of States shall have jurisdiction over all subjects which, according to this Constitution, fall within the competence of the Union and which are not assigned to other Federal authorities.

ARTICLE 85.

The subjects which fall within the sphere of the two Councils are especially the following:

1. Laws pertaining to the organization and mode of selection of the Federal authorities.

2. Laws and decisions upon those subjects whose regulation is entrusted to the Union by the Federal Constitution.

3. Remuneration and compensation of the members of the Federal Official Boards and of the Federal Secretariat: establishment of permanent offices and determination of their salaries.

4. Choice of the Federal Council, of the Federal Tribunal, of the Federal Secretary and of the General of the Federal Army.

The choice or approval of other appointees may by Federal law be entrusted to the Federal Assembly.

5. Alliances and treaties with foreign countries and approval of Cantonal treaties with other Cantons or with

foreign countries. Such Cantonal treaties shall, however, not be submitted to the Federal Assembly unless objection be raised to them by the Federal Council or by another Canton.

6. Measures for external safety, for maintenance of the independence and neutrality of Switzerland, declarations of war and conclusion of peace.

7. Guarantees of the constitutions and territory of the Cantons; intervention in consequence of the guarantee; measures for internal safety, for the establishment of tranquillity and order; amnesty and pardon.

8. Measures for securing observance of the Federal Constitution; the guarantee of the cantonal constitutions, the fulfillment of Federal obligations.

9. Regulations concerning the Federal Army.

10. Establishment of the yearly budget, approval of. public accounts, and decrees as to contracting loans.

11. General supervision of the Federal administration and justice.

12. Appeals from the decisions of the Federal Council in adminstrative disputes.

13. Disputes as to competence among the Federal authorities.

14. Revision of the Federal Constitution.

ARTICLE 86.

Both Councils shall convene once each year in ordinary session on a day to be fixed by regulation.

They may also be summoned in extraordinary session by vote of the Federal Council or on demand of one-fifth of the members of the National Council, or of five Cantons.

ARTICLE 87.

No valid action can be taken in either Council, unless a majority of the members be present.

ARTICLE 88.

In the National Council, and in the Council of States, the majority of those voting shall decide the question.

ARTICLE 89.

For Federal laws and Federal decrees, the consent of both Councils is necessary.

Federal laws, as also general Federal decrees—if not of an urgent nature—must also be submitted to popular vote upon demand of 30,000 qualified voters or of 8 Cantons.

ARTICLE 90.

Necessary details as to forms and times of popular voting shall be fixed by Federal law.

ARTICLE 91.

The members of both Councils vote without instructions.

ARTICLE 92.

The Councils deliberate separately. In case of elections, of granting pardons, and of deciding disputes as to competence (Article 85, 13) the two Councils shall, however, meet in joint session under the chairmanship of the President of the National Council. Votes shall be decided by simple majority of all members of both Councils voting.

ARTICLE 93.

Each Council and every member of each Council shall have the right to make propositions (i. e. have the right of initiative).

The same right belongs to the Cantons by correspondence.

ARTICLE 94.

The sessions of both Councils shall, as a rule, be public.

II.—FEDERAL COUNCIL.

ARTICLE 95.

The supreme executive and directive body of the Confederation shall be a Federal Council consisting of seven members.

ARTICLE 96.

The members of the Federal Council shall be chosen by the Federal Assembly for the term of three years, from among all Swiss citizens who are eligible to the National Council. Not more than one member shall be chosen from the same Canton.

After every general election for the National Council, the Federal Council shall also be integrally renewed.

In cases of vacancy in the meantime in the Federal Council, the vacancies shall be filled for the rest of the term at the next meeting of the Federal Assembly.

ARTICLE 97.

The members of the Federal Council shall not hold any office either in the service of the Union or of a Canton, nor engage in any other calling or business.

ARTICLE 98.

The Federal President who shall preside over the Federal Council shall be chosen, together with the Vice President, for the term of one year, by the Councils in joint session from among their members.

The retiring President is not eligible either as President or Vice President for the next following year. The same member may not hold the office of Vice President for two consecutive years.

ARTICLE 99.

The Federal President and the other members of the

Federal Council shall receive a compensation from the Federal treasury.

ARTICLE 100.

In order to make action valid, four members of the Federal Council must be present.

ARTICLE 101.

The members of the Federal Council shall have the right to take part in the discussions of both branches of the Federal Assembly, and also the right to make motions on any matter under consideration.

ARTICLE 102.

The Federal Council shall have especially the following rights and duties, subject to the provisions of the present Constitution.

1. It shall direct Federal affairs according to Federal laws and decrees.

2. It shall care for the due observance of the Constitution, laws, and decrees of the Union, as well as the provisions of Federal concordats. It shall take the necessary measures for their execution either on its own initiative or upon complaint, so far as the decision of such affairs has not been vested in the Federal Tribunal by Article 113.

3. It shall enforce the guarantee of the Cantonal Constitutions.

4. It shall propose to the Federal Assembly laws and decrees, and shall report upon the propositions sent to it by the Councils of the Union or by the Cantons.

5. It shall execute the Federal laws and decrees, the judgments of the Federal Tribunal, as well as the compromises and arbitrators' decisions on questions of dispute among the Cantons.

6. It shall make such appointments as are not entrusted to the Federal Assembly, Federal Tribunal, or to some other body.

7. It shall examine the treaties of the Cantons with one another or with foreign countries, and shall approve them so far as they are permissible. (Article 85, No. 5.)

8. It shall protect the external interests of the Union especially in all international relations and shall in general have charge of foreign affairs.

9 It shall protect the internal safety, and the independence and neutrality of Switzerland.

10. It shall care for the external security of the Union, and for the establishment of quiet and order.

11. In urgent cases the Federal Council shall have authority, if the Councils are not in session, to call out the necessary number of troops and employ them as it shall see fit: provided that it shall call the Councils together immediately, and provided further that the number of men called out shall not exceed two thousand, nor the term of service exceed three weeks.

12. It shall have charge of Federal army affairs, and all branches of administration which belong to the Union.

13. It shall examine those laws and ordinances of the Cantons which require its approval; and shall watch over those branches of Cantonal administration which are subject to its supervision.

14. It shall manage the finances of the Union, and provide for the preparation of estimates and for a statement of the accounts of Federal income and expenditure.

15. It shall exercise the supervision over the conduct of business by all officers and employees of the Federal administration.

16. It shall report to the Federal Assembly at each ordinary session upon its conduct of business, upon the internal condition and foreign relations of the Union, and shall recommend to its attention such measures as in its judgment are desirable for the promotion of the common welfare.

It shall also make special reports upon the demand of the Federal Assembly or either branch thereof.

ARTICLE 103.

The business of the Federal Council shall be divided according to departments among its various members. The sole purpose of this division is to facilitate the examination and despatch of business. Every decision must emanate from the Federal Council as a body.

ARTICLE 104.

The Federal Council and its departments are authorized to call in the aid of experts for special matters.

III—FEDERAL SECRETARIAT.

ARTICLE 105.

The duties of Secretary to the Federal Assembly and Federal Council, shall be performed by a Federal Secretariat under the direction of a Federal Secretary.

The Secretary shall be chosen for the term of three years by the Federal Assembly, at the same time as the Federal Council.

The Federal Secretariat shall be under the special supervision of the Federal Council.

The details of the organization of the Federal Secretariat shall be determined by Federal law.

IV.—ORGANIZATION AND POWERS OF THE
FEDERAL TRIBUNAL.

ARTICLE 106.

For the administration of justice, so far as it belongs to the Union, a Federal Tribunal shall be organized.

In criminal cases (Article 112) all trials shall be by jury.

ARTICLE 107.

The members of the Federal Tribunal and their substitutes shall be chosen by the Federal Assembly. In this choice care shall be taken that the three national languages shall be represented.

The organization of the Federal Tribunal and of its divisions, the number of its members and substitutes, and their term of office and compensation, shall be determined by law.

ARTICLE 108.

Any Swiss citizen who is eligible to the National Council may be chosen a member of the Federal Tribunal.

The members of the Federal Assembly, or Federal Council, or officers appointed by either of these bodies, shall not at the same time be members of the Federal Tribunal.

The members of the Federal Tribunal shall not hold any other office in the service, either of the Union or of any Canton, nor pursue any other calling or business during their term of office.

ARTICLE 109.

The Federal Tribunal shall organize its own Secretariat.

ARTICLE 110.

The judicial authority of the Federal Tribunal shall extend to civil cases:

1. Between the Union and any Canton.

2. Between the Union and corporations or private persons, when such corporations or private persons are the plaintiffs, and the subject of dispute exceeds a certain value to be fixed by Federal legislation.

3. Between Cantons.

4. Between Cantons and corporations or private persons upon the demand of either party, where the subject of dispute exceeds a certain value to be fixed by Federal legislation.

The Federal Tribunal shall, moreover, pass upon appeals in regard to loss of domicile (Heimathlosigkeit) and upon civil disputes between communes of different Cantons.

ARTICLE 111.

The Federal Tribunal shall, moreover, decide other cases upon the demand of both parties to the suit, when the litigation concerns matters exceeding a certain value to be fixed by Federal legislation.

ARTICLE 112.

With the aid of juries which shall pass upon the facts, the Federal Tribunal shall also decide in criminal cases:

1. Involving high treason against the Union, or revolt or violence against the Federal authorities.

2. Involving crimes and misdemeanors against international law.

3. Involving political crimes or misdemeanors which are the cause or consequence of such disturbances as call for armed intervention on the part of the Union.

4. Involving charges against officials appointed by a Federal authority, upon the application of the latter.

ARTICLE 113.

The Federal Tribunal shall decide further:

1. Disputes as to competence between Federal and Cantonal authorities.

2. Disputes on points of public law between Cantons.

3. Complaints concerning violation of the Constitutional rights of citizens, and appeals of private citizens on account of violation of concordats between Cantons or violation of international treaties.

Administrative disputes, however, (to be more exactly defined by Federal legislation,) shall be excluded from the jurisdiction of the Federal Tribunal.

In all these cases, however, the laws and general decrees

of the Federal Assembly, and the treaties approved by them, shall be the supreme law for the Federal Tribunal.

ARTICLE 114.

Besides the subjects mentioned in Articles 110, 112 and 113, other cases may be placed by Federal law within the competence of the Federal Tribunal. Federal law shall determine, moreover, what powers shall be entrusted to the Federal Tribunal for securing uniformity in the application of such Federal laws as may be passed in accordance with Article 64.

V.—VARIOUS PROVISIONS.

ARTICLE 115.

Federal law shall determine the seat of the Federal authorities.

ARTICLE 116.

The three leading languages of Switzerland, German, French, and Italian, shall be considered national languages of the Union.

ARTICLE 117.

The officials of the Union shall be responsible for their conduct of business. Federal law shall define this responsibility and the means of enforcing it.

THIRD DIVISION.

REVISION OF THE CONSTITUTION.

ARTICLE 118.

The Federal Constitution may be revised at any time.

ARTICLE 119.

Each revision shall take place by the ordinary method of Federal legislation.

ARTICLE 120.

If one branch of the Federal Assembly vote for revision and the other does not approve, or upon the demand of fifty thousand qualified voters—in either case—the question of revision must be submitted to the Swiss people for their decision.

Whenever the majority of citizens voting shall favor revision, both Councils shall be elected anew in order to undertake the revision.

ARTICLE 121.

The revised Constitution shall go into effect whenever it shall receive a majority of all the votes cast and the approval of a majority of the Cantons.

In determining the majority of the Cantons, the vote of each part of a divided Canton shall be counted as half a vote.

The result of the popular vote in each Canton shall be taken as determining the vote of the Canton.

TRANSITION PROVISIONS.

ARTICLE 1.

With respect to the disposition of the revenue from customs and the post, existing provisions shall remain in force until the transfer to the Union of the military burdens now borne by the Cantons shall be completed.

A Federal law shall, moreover, provide that those Cantons which shall suffer financial loss on account of the new arrangements introduced by Articles 20, 30, 36, second clause, and 42 e, shall not be subjected to the entire loss at once, but the loss shall be distributed in a series of years.

Those Cantons which up to the time when Article 20 shall go into effect shall still be in arrears for the military services due under the existing Constitution and laws, shall be required to make good these services at their own cost.

ARTICLE 2.

All provisions of existing Federal laws, of the Concordats of the Cantonal Constitutions and laws, which are in conflict with the new Constitution, become null and void when it shall be accepted, or when the Federal laws passed in pursuance thereof shall be published.

ARTICLE 3.

The new provisions in regard to the powers of the Federal Tribunal shall not take effect until the passage of the Federal laws relating to it.

ARTICLE 4.

The Cantons shall be allowed a period of five years within which to introduce the system of gratuitous public primary schools.

ARTICLE 5.

Persons following one of the learned professions who

may have obtained a certificate of fitness from any Canton, or from any official body representing several Cantons, prior to the passage of the laws indicated in Article 33, shall be entitled to practice their profession throughout the whole Union.

Voted to submit to the people and Cantons by the National Council.

Bern, January 31, 1874,

ZIEGLER, President.

SCHIESS, Keeper of the Minutes.

Voted to submit to the people and Cantons by the council of States.

Bern, January 31, 1874.

A. KOPP, President.

J. L. LÜTSCHER, Keeper of the Minutes.

FEDERAL DECREE

Concerning the result of the vote upon the revised Federal Constitution, submitted January 31, 1874 (of the 29th of May, 1874).

THE FEDERAL ASSEMBLY OF THE SWISS CONFEDERATION.

After examination of the reports of the vote of the Swiss people upon the revised Federal Constitution, submitted January 31, 1874, which vote was taken on April 19, 1874:

After receiving the declarations of the proper Cantonal authorities in regard to the vote of the Cantons on the same subject:

After examination of a message of the Federal Council, dated May 20, 1874,

From which document it appears:

a. That in regard to the popular vote   *   *   *   * 340,199 declared in favor of acceptance, and 198,013 declared against acceptance, leaving a majority of 142,186 in favor of acceptance.

b. That in regard to the vote of the Cantons, 14½ Cantons voted in favor of acceptance, and 7½ voted against acceptance, leaving a majority of 7 Cantons in favor of acceptance.

Hereby declares:

1. That the revised Federal Constitution, submitted by the Federal law of January 31, 1874, has received both the majority of all votes cast, and the approval of a majority of all the Cantons, and that it is, therefore, hereby solemnly declared in effect, bearing date of May 29, 1874.

2. The Federal Council is hereby entrusted with the publication of the present resolution, and with the further measures which may be necessary for its execution.

Voted by the National Council.
     Bern, May 28, 1874.
           ZIEGLER, President.
           SCHIESS, Keeper of the Minutes.

Voted by the Council of States.
     Bern, May 29, 1874.
           A. KOPP, President.
           J. L. LÜTSCHER, Keeper of the Minutes.

———

The Swiss Federal Council enacts:

The foregoing Federal Decree, together with the Swiss Federal Constitution, shall be enrolled in the official collection of Statutes of the Union, and the Decree shall be transmitted to the Governments of the Cantons to be published by them through posting up in public places.

Bern, May 30, 1874.

SHENK, Federal President.
SCHIESS, Federal Secretary.

www.ingramcontent.com/pod-product-compliance
Lightning Source LLC
Chambersburg PA
CBHW021431090426